Are you ready for an Art Attack?

This isn't a book for **fantastic** a⎵⎵ists; this is a book for those ⎵ you who **love** to draw! Drawing is about having fun and th⎵'s what you're going to have!

⎵scover how to **improve** your ⎵toons and drawings with ⎵ple but effective techniques. ⎵ grab yourself some paper and ⎵pencil and turn the page. Let's have an Art Attack!

CONTENTS

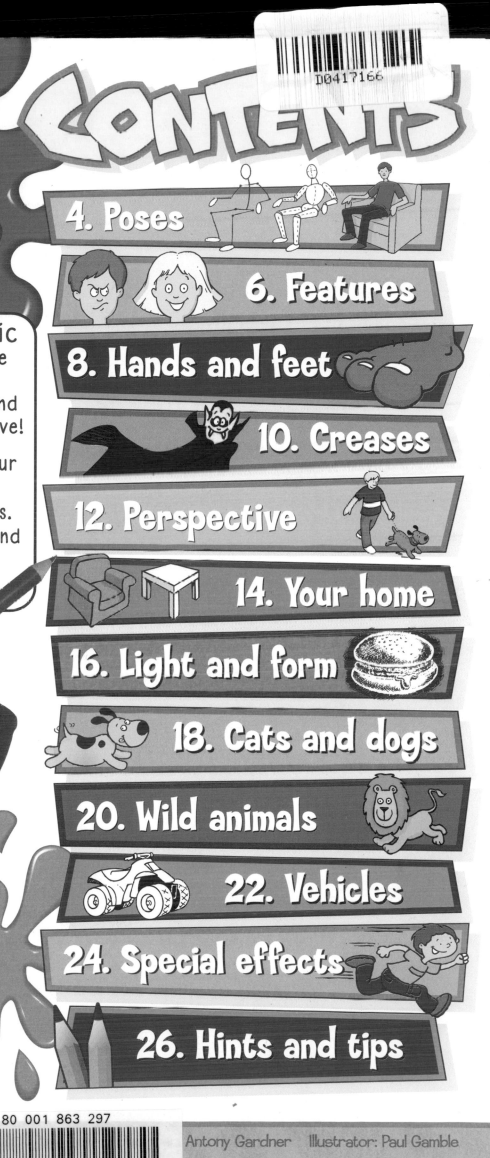

D0417166

80 001 863 297

Antony Gardner   Illustrator: Paul Gamble

How to Draw POSES!

GIVE US A WAVE!

Construct a simple frame or 'skeleton.' Begin with the head and spine. Add shoulders and hips, then limbs. Flesh out your frame with simple shapes and finally add details such as features and clothes.

RUN FOR IT If you need to, get someone to pose for you. Take a close look at how their arms and legs look!

SITTING Keep it simple. Even this sitting pose can be easy to draw!

JUMPING You'll be jumping for joy with your new found drawing skills!

WALKING Try to keep the drawing fluid and relaxed - there's nothing to it!

How to Draw FEATURES!

To draw a profile or three quarters view of a head, start with a circle. Copy the pictures below to find the correct position for the eyes, nose and mouth.

The eyes are round - that's why they're called eye*balls*! The lids follow the eye's rounded shape. The top lid curves more than the bottom lid.

For a three quarters view of a nose, draw a rectangle and a triangle together and then build up the shape like this.

Where the lips meet in the middle, the line is curved.

Cartoon features are even easier to draw! Try these comical expressions!

Draw a portrait from the front, starting with the basic head shape. Eyes should be about half way down the face, the nose is in the middle and the mouth is three quarters the way down.

To draw eyes from the front, draw a flat lemon shape with a circle inside. Add curved lids and a smaller round pupil. Draw eyebrows and colour in the pupil.

Get the basic nose shape by lightly sketching it within a rectangle like this. Noses are slimmer at the top and wider towards the bottom. Add dark ovals for nostrils.

Men's lips are usually longer and narrower than women's lips. Start by drawing one lip at a time.

If you don't want to get serious, have a go at these funny features instead!

How to Draw HANDS & FEET!

VERY HANDY!

Create a hand from simple shapes, starting with a circle. There are 3 main areas: the palm, the thumb and the fingers.

GET A GRIP!

Use 3 dimensional rectangles to get the shape correct. Actually, hands are larger than you think - practice by drawing around your own hands on to paper.

CARTOON CAPERS!

Drawing cartoon hands is easy - they don't even have to have the correct numbers of fingers! Use sausage and egg shapes to create some comical hands.

PUT YOUR FOOT IN IT!

From the side, a foot is wedge shaped with the narrow end being at the ankle.

TIPPY TOES!

Use a rectangle to help you get the proportions right. Draw a slightly wiggly line inside the shape. Add toes and an ankle. Finally erase the rectangle. Get someone to model for you so you can practice!

FUNNY FEET!

Try these for size! Exaggerating certain characteristics is great when cartooning. Take a look at these chunky feet!

9

Creases appear where the material is affected by weight or tension. The arrows illustrate where folds are made as the fabric is being pulled.

Folds may form under the fabric's own weight (see towel above.)

The arrows below indicate from which point the material feels tension and therefore creases or folds.

Some clothes are more bulky than others but they usually follow the shape of the body.

Here are some more poses which show you where creases are made when the body is in different positions.

A few simple lines indicating folds will bring your drawings to life and they make the body look more solid.

Draw a wiggly line. Decide from which point the material hangs (shoulder) and then draw fluid lines from the wiggly line to the shoulder area.

See how shadows form where the folds dip in and the material is lighter where the light falls.

How to Draw PERSPECTIVE!

Drawing in perspective makes things look 3 dimensional on a flat surface like paper.

Vanishing point!

Things gradually get smaller in the distance

THE VANISHING POINT

If you looked down a railtrack the tracks appear to vanish at a point on the horizon. This is called the 'vanishing point.'

However, we mostly view things from an angle where we see more than one side and there is more than one vanishing point. (See below.)

Identical objects such as the trees or people in this picture seem to get smaller and smaller. Drawn correctly these objects add to the illusion of distance.

EYE LEVEL The viewer's eye level is always the horizon line whether the viewer is at the top or the bottom of the ladder.

Eye level and horizon line

Eye level and horizon line

Eye level and horizon line

DIFFERENT VIEWS

Take a look at these objects viewed from three different eye levels. See how the appearance of the object changes depending on whether it's viewed from above, eye level or below.

BOXED OFF

Have a go at building an object or drawing a person within a perspective box or frame. Start by drawing a horizon line and marking your vanishing points. Draw a box and construct your object.

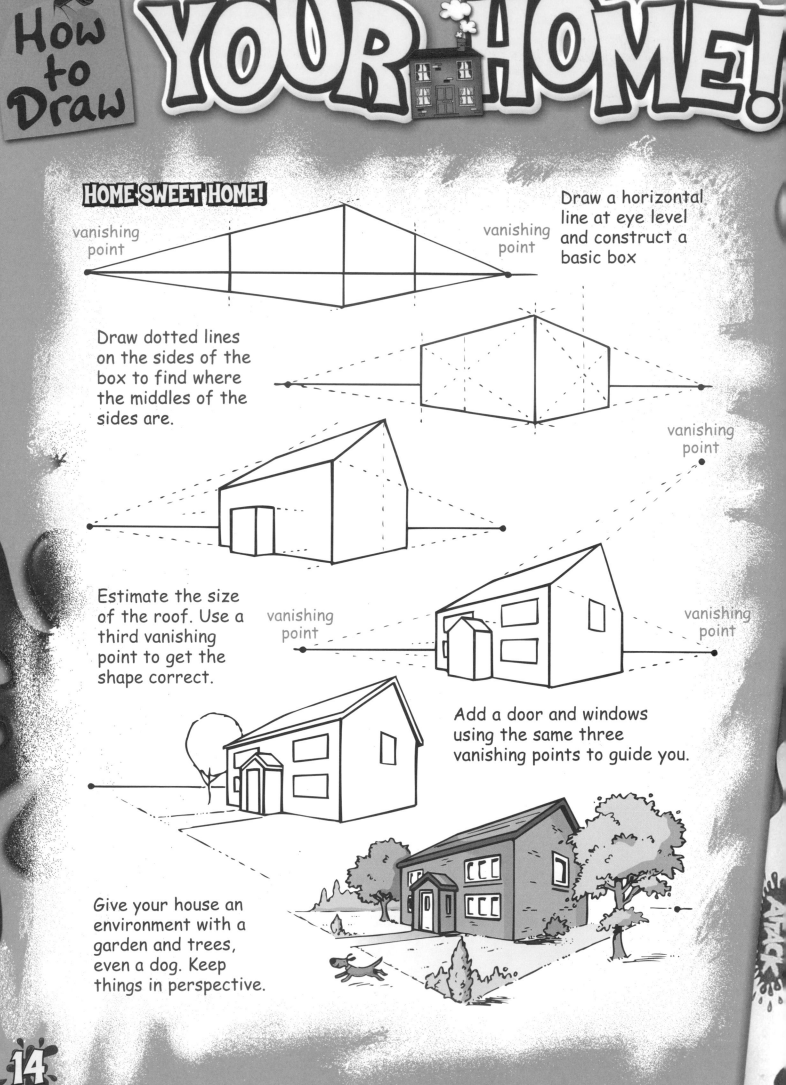

How to Draw YOUR HOME!

HOME SWEET HOME!

vanishing point

vanishing point

Draw a horizontal line at eye level and construct a basic box

Draw dotted lines on the sides of the box to find where the middles of the sides are.

vanishing point

Estimate the size of the roof. Use a third vanishing point to get the shape correct.

vanishing point

vanishing point

Add a door and windows using the same three vanishing points to guide you.

Give your house an environment with a garden and trees, even a dog. Keep things in perspective.

ROOM WITH A VIEW!

Design a room using the principles of perspective.

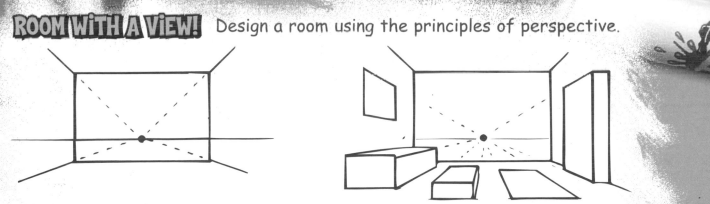

Draw a rectangle with a horizontal line towards the bottom to mark eye level. Add a small dot in the middle as this is your vanishing point.

Using a ruler as a pivot, draw furniture, a rug and pictures. Erase unwanted pencil marks before completing your picture.

BOXED OFF!

Sketch a cube shape and then draw a table and a chair.

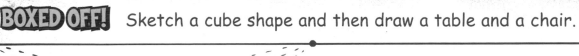

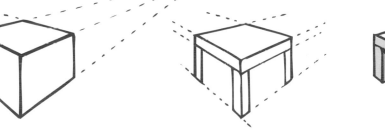

How to Draw LIGHT & FORM!

If there is a light source, objects have shadows. The pictures below show the effect of a moving light source on solid shapes. Can you see how the shadows seem to make the objects look more solid?

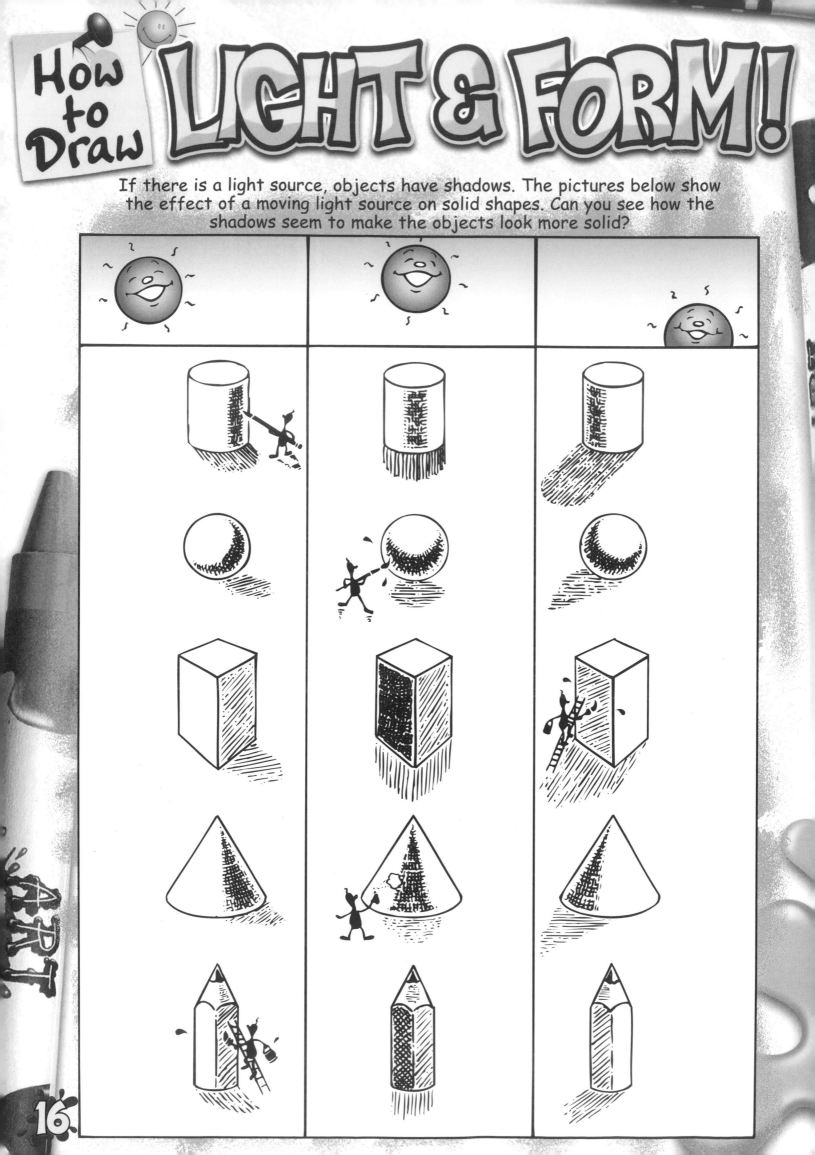

TASTY TREATS

Adding shading (form) to common objects using a strong, single light source makes objects appear more solid.

PEAR SHAPED!

This pear goes from looking flat and plain to a rounded, more realistic looking pear.

FIZZY FUN!

The shadows on this can help to make it look shiny and three dimensional. Apply shadow to the curved areas of the can to create this illusion.

RUGGED RUCKSACK!

See how this technique creates texture on fabric as well?

How to Draw CATS & DOGS!

CAT NAPPING
Circles, ovals and sausage shapes can become a sleepy cat.

CARTOON KITTY
Curved lines and a circle for a head create a leaping cat.

PURRFECT DAY

Start with a wonky triangle and circle for a head. Add the legs and tail before drawing the face.

Now draw a nose, some eyes, the ears and some whiskers.

WALKIES
Use peanut and sausage shapes to draw the perfect puppy!

GOOD BOY
Follow the steps below to draw this cute canine.
Again, use circles and rounded sausage shapes.

Once you've drawn the head, add the body.
Start with the outline and add details later.

SHARK ATTACK!

Start with an oval shape. Add tapered ends, fins and a triangular tail. Finish by colouring it in grey.

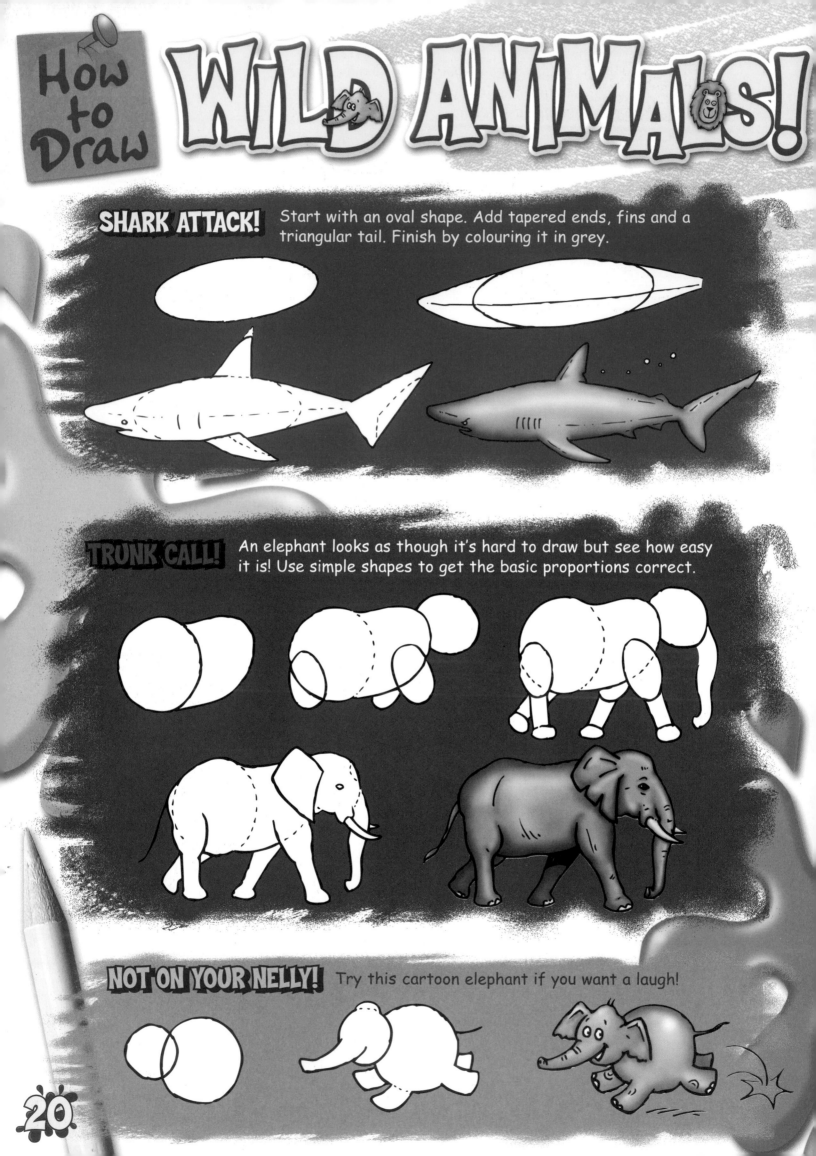

TRUNK CALL!

An elephant looks as though it's hard to draw but see how easy it is! Use simple shapes to get the basic proportions correct.

NOT ON YOUR NELLY!

Try this cartoon elephant if you want a laugh!

WHAT'S UP CROC?

Just like the shark, this crocodile starts as an oval shape. Build the picture up with other shapes, keeping an eraser on hand to remove any unwanted pencil lines.

ROARING SUCCESS!

Draw the king of the jungle by following these steps. When you come to colour him in, create texture in his huge mane by adding some shading.

LOOPY LION!

This cartoon big cat looks a bit more friendly!

How to Draw VEHICLES!

BE A SPORT! Using perspective techniques, draw this cool car. Start by drawing rectangles and carefully build it into this sports car.

WHEELIE COOL! Quad bikes have huge, chunky tyres. Use perspective frames to help you draw them. Use a wedge shape to draw the body part.

ON YER BIKE!

Bikes have 2 equal sized wheels but this one is almost facing forwards. The wheels are more oval and the back one is smaller. The handle bars form a T shape.

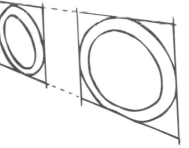

MAD MOTORS!

Have some fun with crazy cartoon cars! Turn over the page to discover what special effects you can add!

How to Draw SPECIAL EFFECTS!

SPEED DEMONS This spaceship is made to look like it's speeding along by adding some cloudy trails coming from the engine.

Give a picture visual energy by adding short 'speed' lines or exaggerate the cartoon by drawing swinging legs in a blur!

The second picture of this skateboarder looks more dynamic due to the whiz lines following his board.

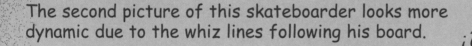

Someone's in a hurry! We can tell by the huge dust trail he's left behind.

CAN YOU KICK IT Establish impact with a flash shape. Make arms and legs swing with some short and longer lines.

WICKED WATER Reflection can be shown in many ways by drawing a mirror image, a small squiggle or waves of light on the water's surface.

Hard, straight black lines can even give an impression of light!

Make a final splash with some huge water drops and a few ripples.

GLOW FOR IT Show shine, glare and sparkle like this..

SINISTER SHADOWS

Add humour and drama with huge shadows produced by strong, low light.

HiNTS AND TiPS!

Everyone can learn to draw, there's no such thing as 'can't!' You don't need much; some paper, pencils and a rubber, and you're away! Below you'll find some suggestions to help you develop those drawing skills.

COMPOSITION!

When you are thinking about drawing a picture it's good to consider the 'composition.' This refers to the layout of the picture. You need to plan where the focal point will be, what will be in the background and how to use the space. To help you, use a 'viewfinder' made from card or paper. Make a simple frame like this one and hold it up to find the composition you are happy to draw.

BE SQUARE!

Another way to improve your drawing skills and help you with harder pictures is to use a grid. If you want to draw from pictures or photos draw a grid of squares on some tracing paper and place it over the picture. Draw another grid on some plain paper. (They must have the same number of squares) Now copy the picture, square by square.

GOING DOTTY!

Rather than using lines to draw, try something different. Create a picture entirely from dots! Start with a dotty outline, then go on to fill in the whole thing with different coloured dots. In fact, if you take a close look at a newspaper, you'll see that the pictures are made up from hundreds of tiny dots.

CREATIVE KIT!

You don't even have to use pencils to draw! Use lots of different materials to draw with; experiment using felt pens, chalk, crayons, ink pen, ball point pen, anything!